Arthur Murphy

Three Weeks after Marriage

A Comedy in two Acts

Arthur Murphy

Three Weeks after Marriage
A Comedy in two Acts

ISBN/EAN: 9783337052270

Printed in Europe, USA, Canada, Australia, Japan

Cover: Foto ©ninafisch / pixelio.de

More available books at **www.hansebooks.com**

Three Weeks after Marriage;

A

C O M E D Y,

In TWO ACTS,

AS PERFORMED AT THE

THEATRE-ROYAL

In COVENT-GARDEN.

———— Otium & oppidi
Laudat rura fui————   Hor.
———— Nugæ feria ducent
In mala————   Hor.

L O N D O N:

Printed and Sold by E. JOHNSON, between No. 4 and 5,
Ludgate Hill.

[PRICE ONE SHILLING.]

ADVERTISEMENT.

THE following Farce was offered to the public in January 1764; but the quarrel about a trifle, and the renewal of that quarrel after the difpute had fubfided, being thought unnatural, the piece was *damned*. Mr. LEWIS of Covent-Garden Theatre, had the good tafte to revive it for his benefit, with an alteration of the title, and it has been fince repeated with fuccefs. A fimilar incident happened to VOLTAIRE at PARIS. That writer, in the year 1734, produced a tragedy, intitled ADELAIDE DU GUESCLIN, which was hiffed through every act. In 1765, LE KAIN, an actor of eminence, revived the play, which had lain for years under condemnation. Every fcene was applauded. What can I think, fays VOLTAIRE, of thefe oppofite judgements? He tells the following anecdote. A banker at Paris had orders to get a new march compofed for one of the regiments of Charles XII. He employed a man of talents for the purpofe. The march was prepared and a practice of it had at the banker's houfe before a numerous affembly. The mufic was found deteftable. MOURET (that was the compofer's name) retired with his performance, and foon after inferted it in one of his operas. The banker and his friends went to the opera; the march was applauded. *Ah; fays the banker, that's what we wanted: why did you not give us fomething in this tafte?* Sir, replied MOURET, the march which you now applaud, is the very fame that you condemned before.

Dra-

Dramatis Perſonæ.

M E N.

Sir CHARLES RACKETT,	Mr. LEWIS.
DRUGGET,	Mr. QUICK.
LOVELACE,	Mr. PALMER.
WOODLEY,	Mr. CUBITT.

W O M E N.

Lady RACKETT,	Mrs. ABINGTON.
Mrs. DRUGGET,	Mrs. PITT.
NANCY,	Mrs. MORTON.
DIMITY,	Mrs. WILSON.

A SERVANT, &c.

Three

Three Weeks after Marriage.

Table. 2 Chairs **ACT I.**

2.   1

Enter Woodley *and* Dimity. *L.H*

Dimity.

PO! Po!------no such thing------I tell you, Mr.
Woodley, you are a mere novice in these affairs.

Wood. Nay, but listen to reason, Mrs. Dimity,---
has not your master, Mr. Drugget, invited me
down to his country-seat, in order to give me his
daughter Nancy in marriage; and with what pretence can he now break off?

Dim. What pretence!------you put a body out of
all patience---But go on your own way, Sir; my
advice is all lost upon you.

Wood. You do me injustice, Mrs. Dimity----
your advice has governed my whole conduct---Have
not I fixed an interest in the young lady's heart?

Dim. An interest in a fiddlestick!------you ought
to have made love to the father and mother---what,
do you think the way to get a wife, at this time of
day, is by speaking fine things to the lady you have
a fancy for?---That was the practice, indeed; but
things are alter'd now---you must address the old
people, Sir; and never trouble your head about

B   your

your miftrefs---None of your letters, and verfes,
and loft looks, and fine fpeeches,----" Have com-
paffion, thou angelic creature, on a poor dying,"
---Pfhaw! ftuff! nonfenfe! all out of fafhion,----
Go your ways to the old curmudgeon, humour his
whims---" I fhall efteem it an honour, Sir, to be
allied to a gentleman of your rank and tafte."
" Upon my word, he's a pretty young gentleman."
-----Then wheel about to the mother: " Your
daughter, Ma'am, is the very model of you, and
I fhall adore her for your fake." " Here, come
hither, Nancy, take this gentleman for better for
worfe." " La, mama, I can never confent."----
" I fhould not have thought of your confent---the
confent of your relations is enough : why, how now,
huffey !" So away you go to church, the knot is
tied, an agreeable honey-moon follows, the charm
is then diffolv'd ; you go to all the clubs in St.
James's Street ; your lady goes to the Coterie ; and,
in a little time you both go to Doctor's Commons ;
and, if faults on both fides prevent a divorce, you'll
quarrel like contrary elements all the reft of your
lives: that's the way of the world now.

Wood. But you know, my dear Dimity, the old
couple have received every mark of attention from
me.

Dim. Attention! to be fure you did not fall afleep
in their company ; but what then ?----You fhould
have entered into their characters, play'd with their
humours, and facrificed to their abfurdities.

Wood. But if my temper is too frank---

Dim. Frank, indeed ! yes, you have been frank
enough to ruin yourfelf.---Have not you to do with
a rich old fhop-keeper, retired from bufinefs with
an hundred thoufand pounds in his pocket, to enjoy
the duft of the London road, which he calls living

in

in the country----and yet you muſt find fault with
h's ſituation !----What if he has made a ridiculous
g'merack of his houſe and gardens, you know his
heart is ſet upon it; and could not you have com-
mended his taſte ? But you muſt be too frank !----
" Thoſe walks and alleys are too regular----thoſe
evergreens ſhould not be cut into ſuch fantaſtic
ſhapes."---And thus you adviſe a poor old me-
chanic, who delights in every thing that's menſtrous,
to follow nature----Oh, you're likely to be a ſuc-
ceſsful lover !

Wood. But why ſhould I not ſave a father-in-law
from being a laughing-ſtock ?

Dim. Make him your father-in-law firſt---

Wood. Why, he can't open his windows for the
duſt---he ſtands all day looking through a pane of
glaſs at the carts and ſtage-coaches as they paſs by,
and he calls that living in the freſh air, and enjoying his own thoughts.

Dim. And could not you let him go on his own
way ? You have ruin'd yourſelf by talking ſenſe to
him, and all your conſenſe to the daughter won't
make amends for it---And then the mother; how
have you play'd your cards in that quarter ?---She
wants a tinſel man of faſhion for her ſecond daugh-
ter---" Don't you ſee (ſays ſhe) how happy my
eldeſt girl is made by marrying Sir Charles Rackett.
She has been married three entire weeks, and not ſo
much as one angry word has paſs'd between them---
Nancy ſhall have a man of quality too."

Wood. And yet I know Sir Charles Rackett perfectly well.

Dim. Yes, ſo do I; and I know he'll make his
lady wretched at laſt---But what then ? You ſhould
have humour'd the old folks,----you ſhould have
been a talking empty fop, to the good old lady,

and

THREE WEEKS

and to the old gentleman, an admirer of his taste in gardening. But you have lost him---he is grown fond of this beau Lovelace, who is here in the house with him; the coxcomb ingratiates himself by flattery, and you're undone by frankness.

Wood. And yet, Dimity, I won't despair.

Dim. And yet you have reason to despair; a million of reasons----To-morrow is fix'd for the wedding-day; Sir Charles and his lady are to be here this very night---they are engag'd, indeed, at a great rout in town, but they take a bed here, notwithstanding.---The family is sitting up for them; Mr. Drugget will keep you all up in the next room there, till they arrive---and to-morrow the business is over----and yet you don't despair !----hush !---- hold your tongue; here comes Lovelace---Step in, and I'll devise something, I warrant you. (*Exit MD* Woodley) The old folks shall not have their own way---'tis enough to vex a body, to see an old father-- and mother marrying their daughter as they please, in spite of all I can do.   [*Exit.*

Enter Drugget and Lovelace.

Drug. And so you like my house and gardens, Mr. Lovelace.

Love. Oh! perfectly, Sir; they gratify my taste of all things. One sees villas where nature reigns in a wild kind of simplicity; but then they have no appearance of art, no art at all.

Drug. Very true, rightly distinguished :----now mine is all art; no wild nature here; I did it all myself.

Love. What, had you none of the great proficients in gardening to assist you ?

Drug. Lackaday! no,---ha! ha! I understand these things---I love my garden. The front of my house, Mr. Lovelace, is not that very pretty ?

Love.

Love. Elegant to a degree!

Drug. Don't you like the fun-dial, plac'd juſt by my dining-room windows?

Love. A perfect beauty!

Drug. I knew you'd like it---and the motto is ſo well adapted---*Tempus edax & index rerum*. And I know the meaning of it----Time eateth and diſcovereth all things---ha! ha! pretty, Mr. Lovelace! ---I have ſeen people ſo ſtare at it as they paſs by--- ha! ha!

Love. Why now, I don't believe there's a noble-man in the kingdom has ſuch a thing.

Drug. Oh no----they have got into a falſe taſte. I bought that bit of ground the other ſide of the road---and it looks very pretty---I made a duck-pond there, for the ſake of the proſpect.

Love. Charmingly imagin'd!

Drug. My leaden images are well---

Love. They exceed ancient ſtatuary.

Drug. I love to be ſurpriz'd at the turning of a walk with an inanimate figure, that looks you full in the face, and can ſay nothing to you, while one is enjoying one's own thoughts----ha! ha!----Mr. Lovelace, I'll point out a beauty to you---Juſt by the haw-haw, at the end of my ground, there is a fine Dutch figure, with a ſcythe in his hand, and a pipe in his mouth---that's a jewel, Mr. Lovelace.

Love. That eſcap'd me: a thouſand thanks for pointing it out---I obſerve you have two very fine yew-trees before the houſe.

Drug. Lackaday, Sir! they look uncouth---I have a deſign about them---I intend---ha! ha! it will be very pretty, Mr. Lovelace---I intend to have them cut into the ſhape of the two giants at Guildhall---ha! ha!

Love.

Love. Exquifite!---why then they won't look like trees.

Drug. Oh, no, no----not at all----I won't have any thing in my garden that looks like what it is---ha! ha!

Love. Nobody underſtands theſe things like you, Mr. Drugget.

Drug. Lackaday! its all my delight now----this is what I have been working for. I have a great improvement to make ſtill---I propoſe to have my evergreens cut into fortifications, and then I ſhall have the Moro caſtle, and the Havanna ; and then near it ſhall be ſhips of myrtle, ſailing upon ſeas of box to attack the town : won't that make my place look very rural, Mr. Lovelace ?

Love. Why you have the moſt fertile invention, Mr. Drugget.

Drug. Ha! ha! this is what I have been working for. I love my garden---but I muſt beg your pardon for a few moments---I muſt ſtep and ſpeak with a famous nurſery-man, who is come to offer me ſome choice things.---Do go and join the company, Mr. Lovelace---my daughter Rackett and Sir Charles will be here preſently---I ſhan't go to bed till I ſee 'em---ha! ha!---my place is prettily variegated---this is what I have been working for ---I fin'd for Sheriff to enjoy theſe things---ha! ha!

[*Exit.*

Love. Poor Mr. Drugget! Mynheer Van Thundertentrunck, in his little box at the ſide of a dyke, has as much taſte and elegance.----However, if I can but carry off his daughter, if I can but rob his garden of that flower——why then I ſhall ſay, " This is what I have been working for." ·

Enter

3

Woodley
Drugget
M.ͬ Drugget

Enter Dimity.

Dim. Do lend us your affiftance, Mr. Lovelace
---you're a fweet gentleman, and love a good na-
tur'd action.

Love. Why how now ! what's the matter ?

Dim. My mafter is going to cut the two yew-
trees into the fhape of two devils, I believe ; and
my poor miftrefs is breaking her heart for it.---Do,
run and advife him againft it---fhe is your friend,
you know fhe is, Sir.

Love. Oh, if that's all---I'll make that matter eafy
directly.

Dim. My miftrefs will be for ever oblig'd to
you ; and you'll marry her daughter in the morning.

Love. Oh, my rhetoric fhall diffuade him.

Dim. And, Sir, put him againft dealing with that
nurfery-man ; Mrs. Drugget hates him.

Love. Does fhe ?

Dim. Mortally.

Love. Say no more, the bufinefs is done. [*Exit.*

Dim. If he fays one word, old Drugget will never
forgive him.---My brain was at its laft fhift ; but if
this plot takes---So, here comes our Nancy.

Enter Nancy. *R. H*

Nan. Well, Dimity, what's to become of me ? ──── *3*

Dim. My ftars ! what makes you up, Mifs ?----I
thought you were gone to bed !

Nan. What fhould I go to bed for ? Only to tum-
ble and tofs, and fret, and be uneafy---they are going
to marry me, and I am frighted out of my wits.

Dim. Why then, you're the only young lady
within fifty miles round, that would be frighten'd
at fuch a thing.

Nan. Ah ! if they would let me chufe for myfelf.

Dim.

Dim. Don't you like Mr. Lovelace?

Nan. My mama does, but I don't; I don't mind his being a man of fashion, not I.

Dim. And, pray, can you do better than follow the fashion?

Nan. ~~Ah! I know there's a fashion for new-born babes, and a fashion for dressing the hair, but~~ I never heard of a fashion for the heart. *Dimity.*

Dim. Why then, my dear, the heart mostly follows the fashion now.

Nan. Does it!---pray who sets the fashion of the heart?

Dim. All the fine ladies in London, o'my conscience.

Nan. And what's the last new fashion, pray?

Dim. Why, to marry any fop that has a few deceitful agreeable appearances about him; something of a pert phrase, a good operator for the teeth, and tolerable taylor.

Nan. And do they marry without loving?

Dim. Oh! marrying for love has been a great while out of fashion.

Nan. Why, then I'll wait till that fashion comes up again.

Dim. And then, Mr. Lovelace, I reckon—

Nan. Pshaw! I don't like him; he talks to me as if he was the most miserable man in the world, and the confident thing looks so pleas'd with himself all the while.-----I want to marry for love, and not for card-playing---I should not be able to bear the life my sister leads with Sir Charles Rackett---and I'll forfeit my ~~new cap~~, if they don't quarrel soon.

Dim. Oh fie! no! they won't quarrel yet awhile.-----A quarrel in three weeks after marriage, would be somewhat of the quickest---By and by we shall hear of their whims and their humours---Well, but

but if you don't like Mr. Lovelace, what say you
to Mr. Woodley?

Nan. Ah!---I don't know what to say--~~but I
can sing something that will explain my mind.~~

S O N G.

WHEN first the dear youth passing by,
    Disclos'd his fair form to my sight,
I gaz'd, but I could not tell why;
    My heart it went throb with delight.

As nearer he drew, those sweet eyes
    Were with their dear meaning so bright,
I trembled, and lost in surprize,
    My heart it went throb with delight.

When his lips their dear accents did try
    The return of my love to excite,
I feign'd, yet began to guess why
    My heart it went throb with delight.

We chang'd the stol'n glance, the fond smile,
    Which lovers alone read aright;
We look'd, and we sigh'd, yet the while
    Our hearts they went throb with delight.

Consent I soon blush'd, with a sigh,
    My promise I ventur'd to plight;
Come, Hymen, we then shall know why
    Our hearts they go throb with delight.

Re-Enter Woodley.

Wood. My sweetest angel! I have heard all, and
my heart overflows with love and gratitude.

Nan. Ah! but I did not know you was listening.
You should not have betray'd me so, Dimity: I
shall be angry with you.

C   *Dim.*

Dim. Well, I'll take my chance for that.---Run both into my room, and say all your pretty things to one another there, for here comes the old gentleman---make haste away.

[*Exeunt* Woodley *and* Nancy. *MD*

Act Begins

Enter Drugget. *LH*

Drug. A forward presuming coxcomb!---Dimity, do you step to Mrs. Drugget, and send her hither.

Dim. Yes, Sir;--- ~~It works upon him, I see.~~ [*Exit. RH*

A

Dimity
Sir Charles

Drug. The yew-trees ought not to be cut, because--- they'll help to keep off the dust, and I am too near the road already---a sorry ignorant sop!---When I am in so fine a situation, and can see every carriage that goes by.----And then to abuse the nursery-man's rarities!---A finer sucking pig in lavender, with sage growing in his belly, was never seen!---And yet he wants me not to have it----But have it I will.---- There's a fine tree of Knowledge, too, with Adam and Eve in juniper; Eve's nose not quite grown, but it's thought in the spring will be very forward--- I'll have that too, with the serpent in ground ivy--- two poets in wormwood---I'll have them both. Ay; and there's a Lord Mayor's feast in honeysuckle; and the whole court of Aldermen in hornbeam ~~and three modern beaux in jessamine, somewhat stunted : they all shall be in my garden~~, with the Dragon of Wantley in box---all---all---I'll have 'em all, let my wife and Mr. Lovelace say what they will---

Enter Mrs. Drugget. *RH*

Mrs. D. Did you send for me, lovey?

Drug. The yew-trees shall be cut into the giants of Guildhall, whether you will or not.

Mrs. D. Sure my own dear will do as he pleases.

Drug. And the pond, tho' you praise the green
banks,

banks, shall be wall'd round, and I'll have a little
fat boy in marble, spouting up water in the middle.

Mrs. D. My sweet, who hinders you?

Drug. Yes, and I'll buy the nursery-man's whole
catalogue---Do you think, after retiring to live all
the way here, almost four miles from London, that
I won't do as I please in my own garden.

Mrs. D. My dear, but why are you in such a
passion?

Drug. I'll have the lavender pig, and the Adam
and Eve, and the Dragon of Wantley, and all of
'em---and there shan't be a more romantic spot on
the London road than mine.

Mrs. D. I'm sure it's as pretty as hands can make
it.

Drug. I did it all myself, and I'll do more----
And Mr. Lovelace shan't have my daughter.

Mrs. D. No! what's the matter now, Mr. Drugget?

Drug. He shall learn better manners than to
abuse my house and gardens.---You put him in the
head of it, but I'll disappoint ye both---And so you
may go and tell Mr. Lovelace that the match is
quite off.

Mrs. D. I can't comprehend all this, not I,---
but I'll tell him so, if you please, my dear---I am
willing to give myself pain, if it will give you plea-
sure: must I give myself pain?---Don't ask me,
pray don't;---I don't like pain.

Drug. I am resolv'd, and it shall be so.

Mrs. D. Let it be so then. (*cries*) Oh! oh!
cruel man! I shall break my heart if the match is
broke off---if it is not concluded to-morrow, send
for an undertaker, and bury me the next day.

Drug. How! I don't want that neither---

Mrs. D. Oh! oh!---

Drug. I am your lord and master, my dear, but not your executioner---Before George, it must never be said that my wife died of too much compliance ---Chear up, my love——and this affair shall be settled as soon as Sir Charles and Lady Rackett arrive.

Mrs. D. You bring me to life again——You know, my sweet, what an happy couple Sir Charles and his lady are——Why should not we make our Nancy as happy?

Enter Dimity.

Dim. Sir Charles and his lady, Ma'am.

Mrs. D. Oh! charming! I'm transported with joy---Where are they? I long to see 'em? [*Exit.*

Dim. Well, Sir; the happy couple are arriv'd.

Drug. Yes, they do live happy indeed.

Dim. But how long will it last?

Drug. How long! don't forbode any ill, you jade---don't, I say---It will last during their lives, I hope.

Dim. Well, mark the end of it---Sir Charles, I know, is gay and good-humour'd---but he can't bear the least contradiction, no, not in the merest trifle.

Drug. Hold your tongue---hold your tongue.

Dim. Yes, Sir, I have done;---and yet there is in the composition of Sir Charles a certain humour, which, like the flying gout, gives no disturbance to the family till it settles in the head---When once it fixes there, mercy on every body about him! but here he comes. [*Exit.*

Enter Sir Charles.

Sir Cha. My dear Sir, I kiss your hand---but why stand on ceremony? To find you up thus late, mortifies me beyond expression. *Drug.*

Drug. 'Tis but once in a way, Sir Charles.

Sir Cha. My obligations to you are inexpressible; you have given me the most amiable of girls; our tempers accord like unisons in music.

Drug. Ah! that's what makes me happy in my old days; my children and my garden are all my care.

Sir Cha. And my friend Lovelace——he is to have our sister Nancy, I find.

Drug. Why my wife is so minded.

Sir Cha. Oh, by all means, let her be made happy ———A very pretty fellow Lovelace————And as to that Mr.———Woodley I think you call him———he is but a plain underbred, ill fashioned sort of a———nobody knows him; he is not one of us———Oh, by all means marry her to one of us.

Drug. I believe it must be so——Would you take any refreshment?

Sir Cha. Nothing in nature—it is time to retire.

Drug. Well, well! good night then, Sir Charles—Ha! here comes my daughter—Good night, Sir Charles.

Sir Cha. Bon repos.

Drug. (*going out*) My Lady Rackett, I'm glad to hear how happy you are, I won't detain you now —there's your good man waiting for you—good night, my girl.   [*Exit.*

Sir Cha. I must humour this old putt, in order to be remember'd in his will.

Enter Lady Rackett.

Lady R. O la!—I'm quite fatigu'd—I can hardly move—why don't you help me, you barbarous man?

Sir Cha. There; take my arm—" Was ever thing so pretty made to walk."

                                        Lady

Lady R. But I won't be laugh'd at—I don't love you.

Sir Cha. Don't you?

Lady R. No. Dear me! this glove! why don't you help me off with my glove! pshaw!———You aukward thing, let it alone; you an't fit to be about me, I might as well not be married, for any use you are of—reach me a chair—you have no compassion for me—I am so glad to sit down—why do you drag me to routs—You know I hate 'em?

Sir Cha. Oh! there's no existing, no breathing, unless one does as other people of fashion do.

Lady R. But I'm out of humour, I lost all my money.

Sir Cha. How much?

Lady R. Three hundred.

Sir Cha. Never fret for that—I don't value three hundred pounds to contribute to your happiness.

Lady R. Don't you?—Not value three hundred pounds to please me?

Sir Cha. You know I don't.

Lady R. Ah! you fond fool!———But I hate gaming---It almost metamorphoses a woman into a fury———Do you know that I was frighted at myself several times to-night———I had an huge oath at the very tip of my tongue.

Sir Cha. Had ye?

Lady R. I caught myself at it---and so I bit my lips———and then I was cramm'd up in a corner of the room with such a strange party at a whist-table, looking at black and red spots---did you mind 'em?

Sir Cha. You know I was busy elsewhere.

Lady R. There was that strange unaccountable woman, Mrs. Nightshade---She behav'd so strangely to her husband, a poor, inoffensive, good-natur'd, good sort of a good for nothing kind of man,———

but

but she so teiz'd him---" How could you play that card ? Ah, youv'e a head, and so has a pin——You're a numscull, you know you are——Ma'am, he has the pocrest head in the world, he does not know what he is about; you know you don't---Ah fye! I'm asham'd of you!"

Sir Cha. She has serv'd to divert you, I see..

Lady R. And then, to crown all---there was my Lady Clackit, who runs on with an eternal volubility of nothing, out of all season, time, and place ---In the very mid'st of the game she begins,——" Lard, Ma'am, I was apprehensive I should not be able to wait on your La'ship---my poor little dog, Pompey---the sweetest thing in the world,---a spade led !---there's the knave---I was fetching a walk, Me'm, the other morning in the Park---a fine frosty morning it was---I love frosty weather of all things---let me look at the last trick---and so, M'em, little Pompey---and if your La'ship was to see the dear creature pinch'd with the frost, and mincing his steps along the Mall---with his pretty little innocent face---I vow 1 don't know what to play---and so, Me'm, while I was talking to Captain Flimsey---Your La'ship knows Captain Flimsey---Nothing but rubbish in my hand---I can't help it ---and so, Me'm, five odious frights of dogs beset my poor little Pompey---the dear creature has the heart of a lion, but who can resist five at once ?---And so Pompey barked for assistance---the hurt he received was upon his chest---the doctor would not advise him to venture out till the wound is heal'd, for fear of an inflamation.---Pray what's trumps ?

Sir Cha. My dear, you'd make a most excellent actress.

Lady R. Well, now let's go to rest---but Sir Charles, how shockingly you play'd that last rubber, when I stood looking over you !

Sir Cha.

Sir Cha. My love, I play'd the truth of the game.

Lady R. No, indeed, my dear, you play'd it wrong.

Sir. Cha. Po! nonfenfe! you don't underftand it.

Lady R. I beg your pardon, I'm allowed to play better than you.

Sir Cha. All conceit, my dear, I was perfectly right.

Lady R. No fuch thing, Sir Charles, the diamond was the play.

Sir Cha. Po! po! ridiculous! the club was the card againft the world.

Lady R. Oh! no, no, no, I fay it was the diamond.

Sir Cha. Zounds! Madam, I fay it was the club.

Lady R. What do you fly into fuch a paffion for?

Sir Cha. 'Sdeath and fury, do you think I don't know what I'm about? I tell you once more, the club was the judgment of it.

Lady R. May be fo——have it your own way, (*walks about and fings*)

Sir Cha. Vexation! you're the ftrangeft woman that ever liv'd; there's no converfing with you——Look'ye here, my Lady Rackett——it's the cleareft cafe in the world, I'll make it plain in a moment.

Lady R. Well, Sir! ha! ha! ha! (*with a fneering laugh*)

Sir Cha. I had four cards left——a trump was led ——they were fix——no, no, no, they were feven, and we nine——then you know——the beauty of the play was to——

Lady R. Well, now it's amazing to me, that you can't fee it——give me leave, Sir Charles——your left hand adverfary had led his laft trump——and he had before finefs'd the club, and rough'd the diamond ——now if you had put on your diamond——

Sir Cha.

λ but you did not get it.

Sir Cba. Zoons! Madam, but we play'd for the odd trick. *I know you plea'd for the odd trick,*

Lady R. ~~And sure the play for the odd trick~~---

Sir Cba. Death and fury! can't you hear me?

Lady R. Go on, Sir.

Sir Cba. Zoons! hear me, I say,---Will you hear me?

Lady R. I never heard the like in my life. [*Hums a tune, and walks about fretfully*]

Sir Cba. Why then you are enough to provoke the patience of a Stoick.---[*looks at her, and she walks about, and laughs uneasily*] Very well, Madam; ---You know no more of the game than your father's leaden Hercules on the top of the house--- You know no more of whist than he does of gardening.

Lady R. Ha! ha! ha! [*Takes out a glass and settles her hair*]

Sir Cba. You're a vile woman, and I'll not sleep another night under one roof with you.

Lady R. As you please, Sir.

Sir Cba. Madam, it shall be as I please---I'll order my chariot this moment---[*Going.*] I know how the cards should be play'd as well as any man in England, that let me tell you---[*Going*]---And when your family were standing behind counters, measuring out tape, and bartering for Whitechapel needles, my ancestors, my ancestors, Madam, were squandering away whole estates at cards; whole estates, my Lady Rackett---[*she hums a tune, and he looks at her*]---Why then, by all that's dear to me, I'll never exchange another word with you, good, bad, or indifferent---Look'ye, my Lady Rackett---thus it stood---the trump being led, it was then my business---

Lady R. To play the diamond, to be sure.

D   *Sir Cba.*

: *Sir Cha.* 'Damn it, I have done with you for ever, and so you may tell your father. [*Exit.* *RH*

Lady R. What a passion the gentleman's in! ha! ha! [*laughs in a peevish manner*] I promise him, I'll not give up my judgment.

Re- *Enter* Sir Charles.

Sir Cha. My Lady Rackett, look'ye, Ma'am— once more, out of pure good-nature—

Lady R. Sir, I am convinc'd of your good-nature.

Sir Cha. That, and that only prevails with me to tell you, the club was the play.

Lady R. Well, be it so---I have no objection.

Sir Cha. It's the clearest point in the world— we were nine, and—

Lady R. And for that very reason:---You know the club was the best in the house.

Sir Cha. There is no such thing as talking to you ---You're a base woman---I'll part from you for ever; you may live here with your father, and admire his fantastical evergreens, till you grow as fantastical yourself---I'll set out for London this instant---[*stops at the door.*] The club was not the best in the house.

Lady R. How calm you are? Well!---I'll go to bed ;---will you come?---You had better--- come then---you shall come to bed---not come to bed when I ask you!---Poor Sir Charles! [*looks and laughs, then exit.* *LD*

Sir Cha. That ease is provoking. [*crosses to the opposite door where she went out*]---I tell you the dia- mond was not the play, and I here take my final leave of you---[*Walks back as fast as he can*] I am resolv'd upon it, and I know the club was not the best in the house. [*Exit.* *RH*

ACT

Chap.

ACT II.

Scene Continues Enter Dimity.

Dimity.

HA! ha! ah! oh! Heavens! I shall expire in
a fit of laughing---this is the modish couple
that were so happy---such a quarrel as they have
had---the whole house is in an uproar---ha! ha!
~~a rare proof of the happiness they enjoy in high~~
~~life. I shall never trust people of fashion mentioned~~
~~again, but I shall be ready to die in a fit of laughter~~
---ho! ho! ho! this is three weeks after marriage,
I think.

Enter Drugget.

Drug. Hey! how! what's the matter, Dimity?
---What am I call'd down stairs for?

Dim Why, there's two people of fashion----
[*stifles a laugh*]

Drug. Why, you saucy minx!---Explain this
moment.

Dim. The fond couple have been together by
the ears this half hour---are you satisfied now?

Drug. Ay!---what have they quarrell'd---what
was it about?

Dim. Something above my comprehension, and
yours too, I believe---People in high life understand their own forms best---And here comes one
that can unriddle the whole affair.   [*Exit.*

Enter Sir Charles.

Sir Cha. [*To the people within*] I say, let the
horses be put to this moment---So, Mr. Drugget.

Drug.

Drug. Sir Charles, here's a terrible bustle—I did not expect this—what can be the matter?

Sir Cha. I have been us'd by your daughter in so base, so contemptuous a manner, that I am determined not to stay in this house to-night.

Drug. This is a thunder-bolt to me! after seeing how elegantly and fashionably you liv'd together, to find now all sunshine vanish'd—Do, Sir Charles, let me heal this breach, if possible.

Sir Cha. Sir, 'tis impossible—I'll not live with her a day longer.

Drug. Nay, nay, don't be over hasty,—let me intreat you, go to bed and sleep upon it—in the morning, when you're cool—

Sir Cha. Oh, Sir, I am very cool, I assure—ha! ha!—it is not in her power, Sir, to—a—a—to disturb the serenity of my temper—Don't imagine that I'm in a passion—I'm not so easily ruffled as you may imagine—But quietly and deliberately I can repay the injuries done me by a false, ungrateful, deceitful wife.

Drug. The injuries done you by a false, ungrateful wife! my daughter, I hope—

Sir Cha. Her character is now fully known to me—she's a vile woman! that's all I have to say, Sir.

Drug. Hey! how!—a vile woman—what has she done—I hope she is not capable—

Sir Cha. I shall enter into no detail, Mr. Drugget; the time and circumstances won't allow it at present——But depend upon it, I have done with her——a low, unpolish'd, uneducated, false, imposing——See if the horses are put-to.

Drug. Mercy on me! in my old days to hear this,

Enter Mrs. Drugget. *S. H*

Mrs. D. Deliver me! I am all over in such a
                                                      tremble

2.

Ld Rackett
Mrs Drugget
Dimity

tremble——Sir Charles, I shall break my heart if
there's any thing amiss.

Sir Cha. Madam, I am very sorry, for your sake
——but there is no possibility of living with her.

Mrs. D. My poor dear girl! What can she have
done ?

Sir Cha. What all her sex can do, the very spirit
of them all.

Drug. Ay! ay! ay!—She's bringing foul dis-
grace upon us——This comes of her marrying a
man of fashion.

Sir Cha. Fashion, Sir!—that should have in-
structed her better—she might have been sensible
of her happiness—Whatever you may think of the
fortune you gave her, my rank in life claims respect
—claims obedience, attention, truth, and love, from
one raised in the world, as she has been by an
alliance with me.

Drug. And let me tell you, however you may
estimate your quality, my daughter is dear to me.

Sir Cha. And, Sir, my character is dear to me.

Drug. Yet you must give me leave to tell you—

Sir Cha. I won't hear a word.

Drug. Not in behalf of my own daughter ?

Sir Cha. Nothing can excuse her—'tis to no pur-
pose—she has married above her; and if that cir-
cumstance makes the lady forget herself, she at least
shall see that I can, and will support my own dignity.

Drug. But, Sir, I have a right to ask—

Mrs. D. Patience, my dear, be a little calm.

Drug. Mrs. Drugget, do you have patience, I
must and will enquire——

Mrs. D. Don't be so hasty, my love; have some
respect for Sir Charles's rank; don't be violent with
a man of his fashion.

Drug. Hold your tongue, woman, I say——
you're

you're not a person of fashion at least——My
daughter was ever a good girl.

Sir Cha. I have found her out.

Drug. Oh! then it is all over—and it does not
signify arguing about it.

Mrs. D. That ever I should live to see this hour!
how the unfortunate girl could take such wickedness
in her head, I can't imagine—I'll go and speak to
the unhappy creature this moment.   [*Exit.* *L.H*

Sir Cha. She stands detected now—detected in
her truest colours.

Drug. Well, grievous as it may be, let me hear
the circumstances of this unhappy business.

Sir Cha. Mr. Drugget, I have not leisure now—
but her behaviour has been so exasperating, that I
shall make the best of my way to town—My mind
is fixed—She sees me no more, and so, your servant, Sir.   [*Exit.*

Drug. What a calamity has here befallen us! a
good girl, and so well dispos'd, till the evil communication of high life, and fashionable vices,
turn'd her to folly.

Enter Lovelace.

Love. Joy! joy! Mr. Drugget, I give you joy.

Drug. Don't insult me, Sir!—I desire you wont.

Love. Insult you, Sir!——is there any thing insulting, my dear Sir, if I take the liberty to congratulate you on—

Drug. There! there!---the manners of high life
for you--he thinks there's nothing in all this——
the ill behaviour of a wife he thinks an ornament to
her character---Mr. Lovelace, you shall have no
daughter of mine.

Love. My dear Sir, never bear malice---I have
reconsidered the thing, and curse catch me, if I

don't

A Song — Sir Charles — Sir Charles — I beg
you will hear me —

follows Sir Charle

go to Page 26

don't think your notion of the Guildhall giants, and
the court of Aldermen in hornbeam---

Drug. Well! well! well! there may be people
at the court end of the town in hornbeam too.

Love. Yes, faith, so there may---and I believe
I could recommend you to a tolerable collection---
however, with your daughter I am ready to venture.

Drug. But I am not ready---I'll not venture my
girl with you---no more daughters of mine shall
have their minds deprav'd by polite vices.

Enter Woodley.

Mr. Woodley---you shall have Nancy to your wife,
as I promis'd you---take her to-morrow morning.

Wood. Sir, I have not words to express---

Love. What the devil is the matter with the old
haberdasher now?

Drug. And hark ye, Mr. Woodley---I'll make
you a present for your garden, of a coronation
dinner in greens, with a champion riding on horse-
back, and the sword will be full grown before April
next.

Wood. I shall receive it, Sir, as your favour.

Drug. Ay, ay! I see my error in wanting an
alliance with great folks---I had rather have you,
Mr. Woodley, for my son-in-law, than any courtly
fop of 'em all. Is this man gone?---Is Sir Charles
Rackett gone?

Wood. Not yet;---he makes a bawling yonder for
his horses---I'll step and call him to you.   [*Exit.*

Drug. I am out of all patience---I am out of my
senses---I must see him once more---Mr. Lovelace,
neither you nor any person of fashion, shall ruin
another daughter of mine.   [*Exit.*

Love. Droll this! damn'd droll! and every syl-
lable of it Arabic to me---the queer old putt is as

whimsical

whimfical in his notions of life as of gardening. If this be the cafe---I'll bruſh, and leave him to his exotics. [*Exit.*

Enter Lady Rackett, Mrs. Drugget, *and* Dimity.

Lady R. A cruel, barbarous man! to quarrel in this unaccountable manner; to alarm the whole houſe, and expofe me and himſelf too.

Mrs. D. Oh, child! I never thought it would have come to this---your ſhame won't end here! it will be all over St. James's pariſh by to-morrow morning.

Lady R. Well, if it muſt be ſo, there's one comfort, the ſtory will tell more to his diſgrace than mine.

Dim. As I'm a ſinner, and ſo it will, Madam. He deſerves what he has met with, I think.

Mrs. D. Dimity, don't you encourage her---you ſhock me to hear you ſpeak ſo---I did not think you had been ſo harden'd.

Lady R. Harden'd do you call it?---I have liv'd in the world to very little purpoſe, if ſuch trifles as theſe are to diſturb my reſt.

Mrs. D. You wicked girl!---Do you call it a trifle to be guilty of falſhood to your huſband's bed?

Lady R. How!---[*Turns ſhort and ſtares at her.*

Dim. That! that's a mere trifle indeed---I have been in as good places as any body, and not a creature minds it now, I'm ſure.

Mrs. D. My Lady Rackett, my Lady Rackett, I never could think to ſee you come to this deplorable ſhame.

Lady R. Surely the baſe man has not been capable of laying any thing of that ſort to my charge---[*Aſide*] All this is unaccountable to me---ha! ha! 'tis ridiculous beyond meaſure.

Dim.

5

3

Sir charles
Dugget

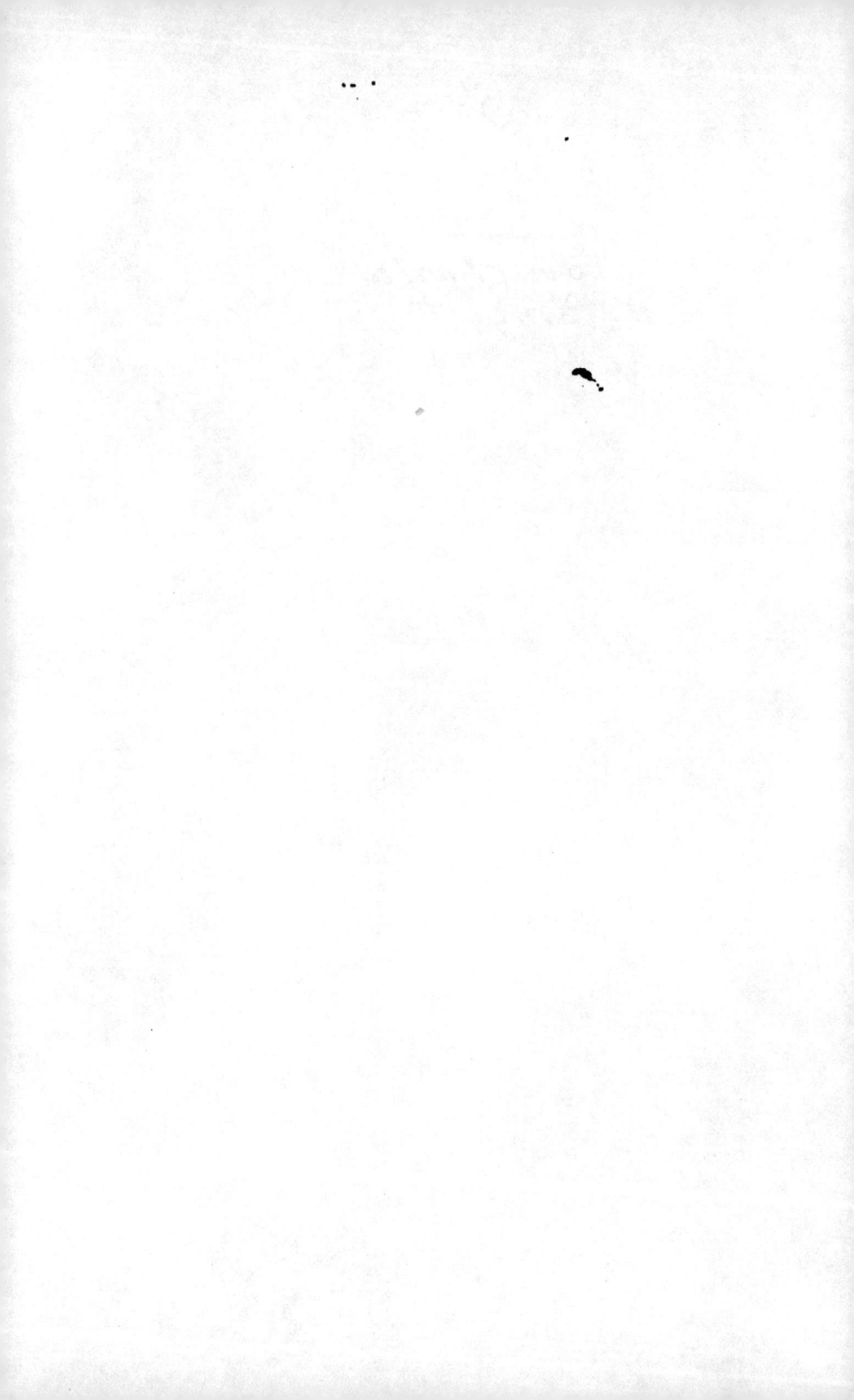

Dim. That's right, Madam:——Laugh at it—
you ferv'd him right.

Mrs. D. Charlotte! Charlotte! I'm aftonish'd
at your wickednefs.

Lady R. Well, I proteft and vow I don't comprehend all this——has Sir Charles accus'd me of any
impropriety in my conduct?

Mrs. D. Oh! too true, he has——he has found
you out, and you have behav'd bafely, he fays.

Lady R. Madam!

Mrs. D. You have fallen into frailty, like many
others of your fex, he fays; and he is refolv'd to
come to a feperation directly.

Lady R. Why then, if he is fo bafe a wretch as
to difhonour me in that manner, his heart fhall ake
before I live with him again.——— *Exit S.*

Dim. Hold to that, Ma'am, and let his head ake
into the bargain.

Mrs. D. Your poor father heard it as well as me.

Lady R. Then let your doors be open'd for him
this very moment——let him return to London——if
he does not, I'll lock myfelf up, and the falfe one
fhan't approach me, tho' he beg on his knees at my
very door, a bafe injurious man! [*Exit.* L H

Mrs. D. Dimity, do let us follow, and hear what
fhe has to fay for herfelf. [*Exit.* L H

Dim. She has excufe enough, I warrant her——
What a noife is here indeed!——I have liv'd in
polite families, where there was no fuch buftle made
about nothing. [*Exit.* L H

Enter Sir Charles *and* Drugget. R H

Sir Cha. 'Tis in vain, Sir, my refolution is taken——

Drug. Well, but confider, I am her father——
indulge me only till we hear what the girl has to
fay in her defence.

E   *Sir*

Sir Cha. She can have nothing to fay——no excufe can palliate fuch behaviour.

Drug. Don't be too pofitive---there may be fome miftake.

Sir Cha. No miftake--did not I fee her, hear her myfelf?

Drug. Lackaday! then I am an unfortunate man!

Sir Cha. She will be unfortunate too---with all my heart---fhe may thank herfelf---fhe might have been happy, had fhe been fo difpos'd.

Drug. Why truly, I think fhe might.

Enter Mrs. Drugget. *I. H*

Mrs. D. I wifh you'd moderate your anger a little---and let us talk over this affair with temper--- my daughter denies every tittle of your charge.

Sir Cha. Denies it! denies it!

Mrs. D. She does indeed.

Sir Cha. And that aggravates her fault.

Mrs. D. She vows you never found her out in any thing that was wrong.

Sir Cha. So! fhe does not allow it to be wrong then!——Madam, I tell you again, I know her thoroughly, I fay, I have found her out, and I am now acquainted with her character.

Mrs. D. Then you are in oppofite ftories—— fhe fwears, my dear Mr. Drugget, the poor girl fwears fhe never was guilty of the fmalleft infidelity to her hufband in her born days.

Sir Cha. And what then?---What if fhe does fay fo!

Mrs. D. And if fhe fays truly, it is hard her character fhould be blown upon without juft caufe.

Sir Cha. And is fhe therefore to behave ill in other refpects? I never charg'd her with infidelity to me, Madam---there I allow her innocent.

Drug.

Drug. And did not you charge her then?

Sir Cha. No, Sir, I never dreamt of fuch a thing.

Drug. Why then, if fhe's innocent, let me tell you, you're a fcandalous perfon.

Mrs. D. Prithee, my dear———

Drug. Be quiet———tho' he is a man of quality, I will tell him of it———did not I fine for fheriff?——— Yes, you are a fcandalous perfon to defame an honeft man's daughter.

Sir Cha. What have you taken into your head now?

Drug. You charg'd her with falfhood to your bed.

Sir Cha. No———never———never.

Drug. But I fay you did———you call'd yourfelf a cuckold———did not he, wife?

Mrs. D. Yes, lovey, I'm witnefs.

Sir Cha. Abfurd! I faid no fuch thing.

Drug. But I aver you did.

Mrs. D. You did, indeed, Sir.

Sir Cha. But I tell you no- politively no.

Drug. and Mrs. D. And I fay yes, pofitively yes———

Sir Cha. 'Sdeath, this is all madnefs———

Drug. You faid fhe follow'd the ways of moft of her fex.

Sir Cha. I faid fo———and what then?

Drug. There he owns it———owns that he call'd himfelf a cuckold———and without rhyme or reafon into the bargain.

Sir Cha. I never own'd any fuch thing.

Drug. You own'd it even now———now———now———now.

Enter Dimity, *in a fit of laughing.*

Dim. What do you think it was all about— ha! ha! the whole fecret is come out, ha! ha!——— It was all about a game of cards——ha! ha!———

E 2

Drug.

Drug. A game of cards!

Dim. (*laughing*) It was all about a club and a diamond. (*runs out laughing*)— *Exit L. H*

Drug. And was that all, Sir Charles?

Sir Cha. And enough too, Sir——

Drug. And was that what you found her out in!

Sir Cha. I can't bear to be contradicted when I'm clear that I'm in the right.

Drug. I never heard such a heap of nonsense in all my life——Woodley shall marry Nancy.

Mrs. D. Don't be in a hurry, my love, this will all be made up.

Drug. Why does not he go and beg her pardon, then?

Sir Cha. I beg her pardon! I won't debase myself to any of you———I shan't forgive her you may rest assur'd. [*Exit.*

Drug. Now there——there's a pretty fellow for you.

Mrs. D. I'll step and prevail on my Lady Rackett to speak to him——then all will be well. [*Exit. L.*

Drug. A ridiculous fop! I'm glad its no worse, however.

Enter Nancy. *L. H*

So Nancy,——you seem in confusion, my girl!

Nan. How can one help it?——With all this noise in the house, and you're going to marry me as ill as my sister——I hate Mr. Lovelace.

Drug. Why so, child?

Nan. I know these people of quality despise us all out of pride, and would be glad to marry us out of avarice.

Drug. The girl's right.

Nan. They marry one woman, live with another, and love only themselves.

Drug.

rugged (SW)

5

Sir Charles — Pack of Cards
Mrs Dorsset

Candles —
&
Pack of Cards } on Table

2 Chairs

$$\frac{b}{}$$
Dogget
L.d Rackett

Drug. And then quarrel about a card.

Nan. I don't want to be a gay lady---I want to be happy.

Drug. And so you shall---don't fright yourself, child---step to your sister, bid her make herself easy ---go, and comfort her, go.

Nan. Yes, Sir. [*Exit. L.H*

Drug. I'll step and settle the matter with Mr. Woodley this moment. [*Exit. R.H*

Enter Sir Charles, *with a pack of cards in his hand.*

Sir Cha. Never was any thing like her behaviour —I can pick out the very cards I had in my hand, and then 'tis as plain as the sun—there—now— there—no—damn it—no—there it was—now let's see—they had four by honours—and we play'd for the odd trick—damnation!—honours were divided ---ay! honours were divided---and then a trump was led---and the other side had the---confusion!--- this preposterous woman has put it all out of my head---[*Puts the cards into his pocket.*] Mighty well, Madam; I have done with you. [*Leaves the cards on the table*

Enter Mrs. Drugget. *L.H*

Mrs. D. Come, Sir Charles, let me prevail—— Come with me and speak to her.

Sir Cha. I don't desire to see her face.

Mrs. D. If you were to see her all bath'd in tears, I am sure it would melt your very heart.

Sir Cha. Madam, it shall be my fault if ever I am treated so again---I'll have nothing to say to her —[*going, stops*] Does she give up the point?

Mrs. D. She does, she agrees to any thing.

Sir Cha. Does she allow that the club was the play?

Mrs. D. Just as you please---she's all submission.

Sir Cha.

Sir Cha. Does she own that the club was not the best in the house?

Mrs. D. She does---she does.

Sir Cha. Then I'll step and speak to her——I never was clearer in any thing in my life. [*Exit.*

Mrs. D. Lord love 'em, they'll make it up now —and then they'll be as happy as ever.

Enter Nancy.

Nan. Well! they may talk what they will of taste, and genteel life——I don't think its natural ——Give me Mr. Woodley——La! there's that odious thing coming this way.

Enter Lovelace.

Love. My charming little innocent, I have not seen you these three hours.

Nan. I have been very happy these three hours.

Love. My sweet angel, you seem disconcerted--- And you neglect your pretty figure---No matter for the present; in a little time I shall make you appear as graceful and genteel as your sister.

Nan. That is not what employs my thoughts, Sir.

Love. Ay, but my pretty little dear, that shou'd engage your attention——to set off and adorn the charms that nature has given you, should be the business of your life.

Nan. Ah! but I have learnt a new song that contradicts what you say, and tho' I am not in a very good humour for singing, yet you shall hear it.

Love. By all means ;---don't check your fancy--- I am all attention.

Nan. It expresses my sentiments, and when you have heard them, you won't teize me any more.

SONG.

S O N G.

To dance, and to drefs, and to flaunt it about,
To run to park, play, to affembly and rout,
To wander for ever in whim's giddy maze,
And one poor hair torture a million of ways:
To put, at the glafs, ev'ry feature to fchool,
And practife their art on each fop and each fool,
Of one thing to think, and another to tell,
Thefe, thefe are the manners of each giddy belle.

To fmile, and to fimper, white teeth to difplay;
The time in gay follies to trifle away;
Againft every virtue the bofom to fteel,
And only of drefs the anxieties feel;
To be at Eye e ear, the infiduous decoy,
The pleafure ne'er tafte, yet the mifchief enjoy,
To boaft of foft raptures they never can know,
Thefe, thefe are the manners of each giddy beau.

[*Exit.*

Love. I muft have her notwithftanding this——
for tho' I'm not in love, yet I'm in debt.

Enter Drugget. *B H*

Drug. So, ~~Sir Lovelace~~ *My dear* any news from above
ftairs? Is this abfurd quarrel at an end---Have they
made it up?

~~Sir Lovel.~~ Oh! ~~a mere bagatelle, Sir~~---thefe little
fracas among the better fort of people never laft
long--~~elegant trifles caufe elegant difputes, and we
come together elegantly again~~---as you fee---for
here they come, in perfect good-humour.

Enter Sir Charles *and* Lady Rackett. *L H*

Sir Cha. Mr. Drugget, I embrace you; Sir, you
fee me now in the moft perfect harmony of fpirits.

Drug.

Drug. What, all reconcil'd again?

Lady R. All made up, Sir---I knew how to bring him to my lure---This is the first difference, I think, we ever had, Sir Charles.

Sir Cha. And I'll be sworn it shall be the last.

Drug. I am happy at last---Sir Charles, I can spare you an image to put on the top of your house in London.

Sir Cha. Infinitely oblig'd to you.

Drug. Well! well!---It's time to retire now--- I am glad to see you reconciled---and now I'll wish you a good night, ~~Sir Charles. My Lord, this is your way after you well both--- I am glad your quarrels are at an end--- This way, My Lord.~~   [*Exeunt* ~~Lovelace and~~ Drugget.

Lady R. Ah! you're a sad man, Sir Charles, to behave to me as you have done.

Sir Cha. My dear, I grant it---and such an absurd quarrel too---ha! ha!

~~Lady R. Yes---ha! ha!---about such a trifle.~~

Sir Cha. It's pleasant how we could both fall into such an error---ha! ha!

~~Lady R. Ridiculous beyond expression---ha! ha!~~

Sir Cha. And then the mistake your father and mother fell into---ha! ha!

Lady R. That too is a diverting part of the story---ha! ha!---But, Sir Charles, must I stay and live with my father till I grow as fantastical as his own evergreens.

Sir Cha. No, no, prithee---don't remind me of my folly.

Lady R. Ah! my relations were all standing behind counters, selling Whitechapel needles, while your family were spending great estates.

Sir Cha. Nay, nay, spare my blushes.

Lady R.

Sir Charles take care of your lady — & I'll
& comfort my old woman.
^ and Mr.ˢ Dagget — R.H

7

Servant — with slippers

Lady R. How could you fay fo harfh a thing ?
---I don't love you.

Sir Cha. It was indelicate, I grant it.

Lady R. Am I a vile woman ?

Sir Cha. How can you, my angel ?

Lady R. I fhan't forgive you!---I'll have you on
your knees for this. (*fings and plays with him*)---
" Go, naughty man."---Ah ! Sir Charles !

Sir Cha. The reft of my life fhall aim at con-
vincing you how fincerely I love---

Lady R. (*fings*) " Go, naughty man, I can't
abide you."---Well ! come let us go to reft. (*going*)
Ah, Sir Charles !---now it is all over, the diamond
was the play.

Sir Cha. Oh no, no, no,---my dear ! ha ! ha !---
it was the club indeed.

Lady R. Indeed, my love, you're miftaken.

Sir Cha. Oh, no, no, no.

Lady R. But I fay, yes, yes, yes---[*Both laughing*]

Sir Cha. Pfhaw ! no fuch thing---ha ! ha !

Lady R. 'Tis fo, indeed---ha ! ha !

Sir Cha. No, no, no---you'll make me die with
laughing.

Lady R. Ay, and you make me laugh too---
ha ! ha ! (*toying with him*)

Enter Footman.

Footm. Your honour's flippers.

Sir Cha. Ay,
take thefe fhoes off [*he takes 'em off, and leaves 'em
at a diftance*] Indeed my Lady Rackett, you make
me ready to expire with laughing---ha ! ha !

Lady R. You may laugh---but I'm right, notwithftanding.

Sir Cha. How can you fay fo ?

Lady R. How can you fay otherwife ?

F   *Sir Cha.*

Sir Cba. Well now mind me, my Lady Rackett
---We can now talk of this matter in good humour
---We can difcufs it coolly--- ~~dit when with down~~

Lady R. So we can---and it's for that reafon I
venture to fpeak to you---are thefe the ruffles I
bought for you?

Sir Cba. They are, my dear.

Lady R. They are very pretty---but indeed you
played the card wrong.

Sir Cba. Po, there is nothing fo clear---if you
will but hear me---only hear me.

Lady R. Ah!---but do you hear me---the thing
was thus---the adverfary's club being the beft in
the houfe—

Sir Cba. How can you talk fo!---[*fomewhat
peevifh*

Lady R. See there now—

Sir Cba. Liften to me---this was the affair---

Lady R. Pfhaw! fiddleftick! hear me firft.

Sir Cba. Po---no---damn it, let me fpeak.

Lady R. Well, to be fure you're a ftrange man.

Sir Cba. Plague and torture! there is no fuch
thing as converfing with you.

~~*Lady R.* Very well, Sir I fly out again~~

Sir Cba. Look here now, ~~here's a pack of cards~~
---now you fhall be convinc'd--- *hone are the very* ~~la~~

~~*Lady R.* You may talk till to morrow, I know~~
I'm right. [*walks about*]

Sir Cba. Why then, ~~by all~~ that's perverfe, you
~~are the moft headftrong---Can you look here now~~
~~------here are the very~~ cards.

Lady R. Go on; you'll find it out at laft.

Sir Cba. Damn it! will you let a man fhew you.
~~Po! it's all nonfenfe---I'll talk no more about it~~
~~--[puts up the cards] Come, we'll go to bed.~~
~~[going]~~

5

Mr & Mrs Drugget

~~Lovel~~

. Woodley & Nancy

(He goes to the table) There are the very same
cards I held in my hand.5.

A You see my love — these were my cards — it was
my lead — then I play'd that card —
Lady &c — Yes. my love — I know you play'd
that card — but you shou'd have play'd
that card.

[~going~] Now only ſtay a moment--- [~takes out the~
~cards~] Now, mind me---ſee here---

Lady R. No, it does ~not~ ſignify---your head
will be clearer in the morning---I'll go to bed.

Sir Cha. Stay a moment, can't ye.

~Lady R. No---my head begins to ake---[affectedly]~

Sir Cha. Why then, damn the cards----there---
there [*throwing the cards about*] And there, and
there---You may go to bed by yourſelf ; and con-
fuſion ſieze me, if I live a moment longer with you
---[*Putting on his ſhoes again*]

~Enter Dimity.~

~Dim. Did you call, Sir ?~

Sir Cha. No, never, Madam.

~Dim. (in a fit of laughing) What, at it again.~

Lady R. Take your own way, Sir.

Sir Cha. Now then, I tell you once more you are
a vile woman.

~Dim. Law, Sir !---This is charming---I'll run~
and tell the old couple.   [*Ex.*

Sir Cha. (*ſtill putting on his ſhoes*) You are the
moſt perverſe, obſtinate, nonſenſical---

Lady R. Ha ! ha ! don't make me laugh again,
Sir Charles.

Sir Cha. Hell and the devil----Will you ſet
down quietly, and let me convince you.

Lady R. I don't chuſe to hear any more about it.

Sir Cha. Why then I believe you are poſſeſſed---
it is in vain to talk ſenſe and reaſon to you.

Lady R. Thank you for your compliment, Sir---
ſuch a man [*with a ſneering laugh*] I never knew
the like---[*ſits down*]

Sir Cha. I promiſe you, you ſhall repent of this
uſage, before you have a moment of my company
again---it ſhan't be in a hurry you may depend,

Lady Rackitt— Ha. ha. ha.

~~Madam—Now see here—I can prove it to a de-~~
~~monstration~~ [*sits down by her, she gets up*] Look ye
there again now——~~you have the most perverse and~~
~~peevish temper~~---I wish I had never seen your face
---I wish I was a thousand miles off from you——
~~sit down but one moment.~~

Lady R. I'm dispos'd to walk about, Sir.

Sir Cha. Why then, may I perish if ever—a
blockhead—an ideot I was to marry [*walks about*]
such a provoking—impertinent—[*she sits down*]
Damnation!—I am so clear in the thing—she is not
worth my notice---[*sits down, turns his back, and
looks uneasy*] I'll take no more pains about it---
[*Pauses for some time, then looks at her*] Is not it
very strange that you won't hear me?

Lady R. Sir, I am very ready to hear you.

Sir Cha. Very well then---very well---my dear
---you remember how the game stood.

Lady R. I wish you'd untie my necklace, it
hurts me.

Sir Cha. Why can't you listen?

Lady R. I tell you it hurts me terribly.

~~Sir Cha. Death and confusion! there is no bear-~~
~~ing this~~---you may be as wrong as you please, and
may I never hold four by honours, if I ever endea-
vour to set you right again.   [*Exit.*

R H Enter Mr. *and* Mrs. Drugget, Woodley, ~~Lovelace~~
and Nancy. *L H*

Drug. What's here to do now?

Lady R. Never was such a man born---I did not
say a word to the gentleman---and yet he has been
raving about the room like a madman.

Drug And about a club again, I suppose.—
Come hither, Nancy; Mr. Woodley, she is yours
for life.

                              Mrs. D.

∧ In running off R.H— he drives against

Mr & Mrs Doggett as they are entering

§: I wish he was put to bed with a spade

Mrs. D. My dear, how can you be so---

Drug. It shall be so---take her for life, Mr. Woodley.

Wood. My whole life shall be devoted to her happiness.

~~*Lott.* The devil! and so I am to be left in the~~ lurch in this manner, am I?

Lady R. Oh! this is only one of those polite disputes which people of quality, who have nothing else to differ about, must always be liable to---This will all be made up.

Drug. ~~Never tell me---it's too late now~~---Mr. Woodley, I recommend my girl to your care---I shall have nothing now to think of, but my greens, and my images, and my shrubbery---though, mercy on all married folks, say I! for these wranglings are, I am afraid, *What we must all come to.*

Lady Rackett *coming forward.*

WHAT we must all come to? *What?---Come to what?*
Must broils and quarrels be the marriage lot?
If that's the wise, deep meaning of our poet,
The man's a fool! a blockhead! and I'll shew it.
~~*What could induce him to engage so wise,*~~
So fam'd for virtue, so refin'd from vice,
To form a plan so trivial, false, and low?
As if a belle could quarrel with a beau:
As if there were---in these thrice happy days,
One who from nature, or from reason strays!
There's no cross husband now; no wrangling wife;
The man is downright ignorant of life.
'Tis the millennium this---devoid of guile,
~~*Fair gentle truth, and white rob'd candour smile.*~~

From

From every breaſt the ſordid love of gold
Is baniſh'd quite---no boroughs now are ſold!
Pray tell me, Sirs---[for I don't know I vow,]
Pray---is there ſuch a thing as Gaming now?
Do peers make laws againſt that giant vice?
And then at Arthur's break them in a trice?
No---no---our lives are virtuous all, auſtere and hard;
Pray, Ladies---do you ever ſee a card?
Thoſe empty boxes ſhew you don't love plays;
The managers, poor ſouls! get nothing now a days.
If here you come---by chance but once a week,
The pit can witneſs that you never ſpeak:
Penſive Attention ſits with decent mien;
No paint, no naked ſhoulders to be ſeen!

And yet this grave, this moral, pious age,
Has learn one uſeful leſſon from the ſtage.
Shun ſtrife, ye fair, and once a conteſt o'er,
Wake to a blaze the dying flame no more:
From fierce debate, fly all the tender loves,
And Venus cries " Coachman put-to my doves,"
The genial bed no blooming Grace prepares,
" And every day becomes a day of cares."

F I N I S.

www.ingramcontent.com/pod-product-compliance
Lightning Source LLC
Chambersburg PA
CBHW021531090426
42739CB00007B/888